The Autumn-Time Cookbook

Delicious Autumn Recipes for when the Leaves Change Colors

By
BookSumo Press
All rights reserved

Published by
http://www.booksumo.com

Table of Contents

Squash and Cilantro Soup 5

Chicken Soup 6

Chowder I 7

Squash Lasagna 8

Easy Stir Fried Squash 9

Italian Inspired Squash 10

Mediterranean Inspired Squash 11

Squash for Autumn 12

Szechwan Shrimp 13

Basil Shrimp 14

Shiitake and Potatoes 15

Japanese Mushroom Soup I 16

Japanese Mushroom Soup II 17

Rustic Beef with Mushroom Sauce 18

Elegant Shiitake and Pasta 19

October's Lo-Mein 20

Herbed Dumplings 21

Rhubarb Dumplings 22

Mexi-Melt 23

Cream of Hash Browns Casserole 24

Buttery Celery and Carrots 25

Creamed Corn Bread Casserole 26

Pumpkin Bread I 27
Pumpkin Pie II 28
Pumpkin Soup I 29
Pumpkin Chili I 30
Pumpkin Curry II 31
Pumpkin & Chicken 32
Cranberry Salad 33
Spinach Salad 34
Crock Pot Oatmeal I 35
Cranberry Maple Oatmeal 36
Balsamic Mushroom Sandwich 37
Meat Loaf with Oats 38
Irish Apple Mash 39
Thanksgiving Favorite Apple Dessert 40
Traditional Autumn Sweet Treat 41
Refreshing Apple Juice 42
Shrimp Tempura 43
Cloves, Allspice, and Cinnamon Chili 44
November 3 Bean Chili 45
Backroad Chili 46
Chicken & Veggies Spring Rolls 47
Banana & Brown Sugar Spring Rolls 48
Shrimp & Veggies Spring Rolls with Dipping Sauce 49
Apple Dumplings 50

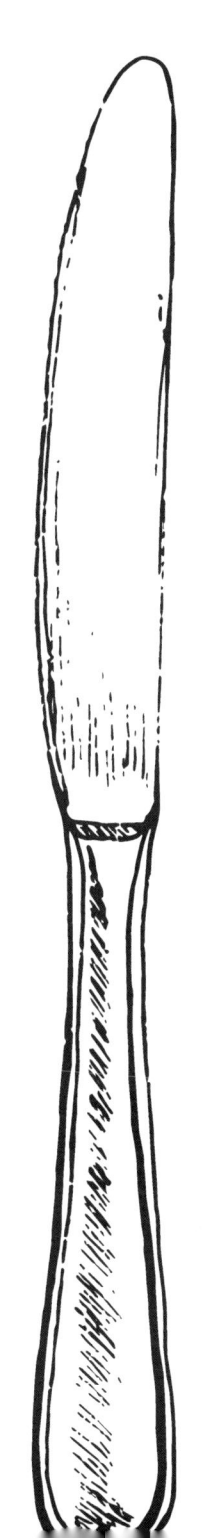

Elegant Apple & Cheddar Stuffed Chicken Breast 51
Easiest Apple Crisp 52
Autumn Muffins 53
Countryside Baked Chicken 54
Turkey Pot Pie 55
Au Gratin 56
Creamy Mashed Potatoes 57
Buttery Quinoa 58
Feta, Peppers, and Lime Quinoa Salad 59
Mushroom and Chard Quinoa 60
November's Quinoa 61

Squash and Cilantro Soup

Prep Time: 30 mins
Total Time: 1 hr

Servings per Recipe: 4
Calories   61 kcal
Fat   3.2 g
Cholesterol   8 mg
Sodium   604 mg
Carbohydrates 7.7 g
Protein   1.6 g

Ingredients

- 2 cubes chicken bouillon, crumbled
- 2 C. hot water
- 1 tbsp unsalted butter
- 1 small yellow onion, minced
- 3 cloves garlic, minced
- 1/4 tsp mashed red pepper flakes
- 2 chayote squashes, peeled and cut into 1/2-inch pieces
- 2 tbsps chopped fresh cilantro
- salt and ground black pepper to taste
- 1 tbsp chopped fresh cilantro

Directions

1. Cook onion, red pepper and garlic in hot butter for a few mins and add the squash, 2 tbsps cilantro, salt, and pepper before cooking it for another 5 mins.
2. Now stir in bouillon (which was dissolved in hot water) and cilantro before cooking all this on low heat for 20 mins.
3. Blend the mixture in a blender until smooth.
4. Serve in bowls.

CHICKEN SOUP (Countryside Style)

🥣 Prep Time: 5 mins
🕐 Total Time: 25 mins

Servings per Recipe: 8
Calories   462 kcal
Fat   36.5 g
Cholesterol   135 mg
Sodium   997 mg
Carbohydrates   22.6 g
Protein   12 g

Ingredients

4 C. chicken broth
2 C. water
2 cooked, boneless chicken breast halves, shredded
1 (4.5 oz.) package quick cooking long grain and wild rice with seasoning packet
1/2 tsp salt
1/2 tsp ground black pepper
3/4 C. all-purpose flour
1/2 C. butter
2 C. heavy cream

Directions

1. Bring a mixture of broth, chicken and water to boil and add rice before turning off the heat and covering it up.
2. Cook content of seasoning packet in hot butter until bubbly before turning down the heat to low and stirring a mixture of salt, pepper and flour.
3. Now add cream and cook for another 5 mins.
4. Now pour this cream mixture into the rice mixture before cooking it over medium heat for about 15 mins.
5. Serve.

Chowder I
(New England Style)

Prep Time:	20 mins
Total Time:	50 mins
Servings per Recipe:	4
Calories	526 kcal
Fat	30.8 g
Cholesterol	98 mg
Sodium	763 mg
Carbohydrates	47.2 g
Protein	16.3 g

Ingredients

- 4 slices turkey bacon
- 1/2 C. chopped onion
- 4 potatoes, peeled and cubed
- 1 tbsp all-purpose flour
- 1 C. bottled clam juice
- 1 C. half-and-half
- 2 (6 oz.) cans minced clams
- salt and pepper to taste
- 1/2 C. heavy cream (optional)
- 2 tbsps chopped fresh parsley

Directions

1. Cook bacon over medium heat for 10 mins before crumbling it and setting it aside.
2. Now cook onion and potatoes for 5 mins before stirring in flour and mixing it well.
3. Now add clam juice and bring all this to a boil before cooking on low heat for 15 mins.
4. Stir in half-and-half, minced clams, salt, pepper and heavy cream before cooking for 5 more mins.
5. Sprinkle some parsley and crumbled bacon for the garnishing purpose.

SQUASH
Lasagna

🥣 Prep Time: 30 mins
🕐 Total Time: 1 hr 45 mins

Servings per Recipe: 6
Calories   280 kcal
Fat   15.9 g
Carbohydrates   24.5g
Protein   14.1 g
Cholesterol   27 mg
Sodium   1294 mg

Ingredients

1 spaghetti squash, halved lengthwise and seeded
1 onion, chopped
2 tbsps minced garlic
2 (14 oz.) cans stewed tomatoes
1 tbsp dried basil
1 cube vegetable bouillon
black pepper to taste
1 (15 oz.) can black olives, chopped
1 C. shredded mozzarella cheese
1 C. shredded Parmesan cheese

Directions

1. Coat a casserole dish with non-stick spray and then set your oven to 325 degrees before doing anything else.
2. Cook the squash in the oven for 37 mins then take everything out of the oven.
3. Shred the flesh and place it in a bowl. But keep the rinds as well separate.
4. Stir fry your garlic and onions in a pan with nonstick spray until browned and then add in: black pepper, tomatoes, bouillon, and basil.
5. Let this cook for 17 mins.
6. Layer the following in the squash rinds: tbsp of tomatoes mix, squash, mozzarella, olive.
7. Continue layering until all the rinds are full. Now top with some parmesan.
8. Once all your ingredients have been layered cook everything in the oven for 22 mins. Enjoy.

Easy Stir Fried Squash

🥣 Prep Time: 15 mins
🕐 Total Time: 15 mins

Servings per Recipe: 4	
Calories	165 kcal
Fat	12.5 g
Carbohydrates	14.2 g
Protein	1.5 g
Cholesterol	31 mg
Sodium	113 mg

Ingredients

- cooking spray
- 1 spaghetti squash, halved and seeded
- 1/4 C. butter or margarine
- 1 small onion, chopped
- 2 cloves garlic, finely chopped
- salt and pepper to taste

Directions

1. Grease a casserole dish with non-stick spray and then set your oven to 350 degrees before doing anything else.
2. Cook your squash in the oven for 42 mins.
3. Then let it loose its heat before scraping out the insides with a fork and placing everything to the side. Now throw away the rinds.
4. Stir fry your onions and garlic in butter until tender and then pour in your squash and continue cooking it until it is warm. Now top everything with some pepper and salt.
5. Enjoy.

ITALIAN INSPIRED
Squash

Prep Time: 10 mins
Total Time: 1 hr 50 mins

Servings per Recipe: 6
Calories 154 kcal
Fat 7.6 g
Carbohydrates 10.3g
Protein 11.3 g
Cholesterol 44 mg
Sodium 99 mg

Ingredients

1 small spaghetti squash, halved and seeded
1 tbsp olive oil
1/2 C. minced onion
3 cloves garlic, minced
2 green onions, minced
12 oz. ground white meat turkey
2 C. crushed tomatoes
2 tbsps water
2 tsps capers
2 tsps minced fresh oregano
2 tsps crushed red pepper flakes
2 tbsps chopped fresh parsley

Directions

1. Set your oven to 350 degrees before doing anything else.
2. Cook your squash in the oven for 47 mins then once it has cooled shred out the insides with a fork and place everything in a bowl to the side.
3. Stir fry your onions, scallions, and garlic for 4 mins then combine in your turkey and continue for 5 more mins.
4. Add the water and tomatoes and get everything boiling then set the heat to low and let the contents gently boil for 22 mins.
5. After 22 mins add in: parsley, capers, red pepper flakes, and oregano.
6. Continue gently boiling for 7 more mins.
7. Heat your squash again if it is completely cold and then place a layer of turkey sauce over it before serving.
8. Enjoy.

Mediterranean Inspired Squash

Prep Time: 15 mins
Total Time: 1 hr 15 mins

Servings per Recipe:	2
Calories	367 kcal
Fat	14.7 g
Carbohydrates	52.9 g
Protein	15.5 g
Cholesterol	22 mg
Sodium	364 mg

Ingredients

- 1 (2 1/2 lb) spaghetti squash, halved lengthwise and seeded
- cooking spray
- salt and ground black pepper to taste
- 1 tsp olive oil, or as needed
- 1/4 Spanish onion, diced
- 1 bunch fresh asparagus, cut into 1-inch pieces
- 2 cloves garlic, minced
- 1/2 C. vegetable broth
- 2 oz. goat cheese
- 2 tbsps chopped fresh basil
- 1 tbsp minced fresh thyme

Directions

1. Coat a casserole dish with foil and then set your oven to 400 degrees before doing anything else.
2. Coat your squash with some pepper and salt and then some nonstick spray and cook everything in the oven for 40 mins.
3. Now let it loose its heat before shredding the flesh and discarding the seeds and rinds.
4. Now place everything in a bowl.
5. Stir fry your onions in olive oil for 7 mins then add in your asparagus and cook for 6 more mins.
6. Now add the garlic and cook for 2 more mins. Place the mix on a plate.
7. Add your squash to the pan and cook for 4 mins then add in your broth and get everything gently boiling with medium to low heat.
8. Cook the broth for 3 mins then add the cheese and onions into the mix and cook for 2 more mins.
9. Season everything with pepper, basil, salt, and thyme.
10. Enjoy.

SQUASH
for Autumn

🥣 Prep Time: 20 mins
🕐 Total Time: 1 hr 30 mins

Servings per Recipe: 7
Calories   166 kcal
Fat   3.6 g
Carbohydrates   28.6g
Protein   5.5 g
Cholesterol   0 mg
Sodium   572 mg

Ingredients

- 1 onion, chopped
- 3 cloves crushed garlic
- 1 tbsp olive oil
- 1 1/2 tsps curry powder
- 1 tsp ground cumin
- 1 tsp ground turmeric
- 8 C. vegetable stock
- 1/4 C. dry lentils
- 1 (28 oz.) can diced tomatoes with juice
- 1/4 C. uncooked white rice
- 1 C. frozen corn
- 1/4 C. elbow macaroni
- 1 small spaghetti squash

Directions

1. Set your oven to 350 degrees before doing anything else.
2. Cook your squash in the oven for 35 mins then shred the flesh and remove the seeds and rinds.
3. In olive oil, in a big pot, cook your garlic and onions for 3 mins, then add: turmeric, curry, and cumin.
4. Cook or 2 more mins before adding the lentils and stock.
5. Get everything boiling.
6. Once it is all boiling, lower the heat to a gentle simmer, and pour in your tomatoes and juice.
7. After 27 mins add in the white rice and the corn and then after 35 mins combine in the squash and macaroni.
8. Let the contents continue to simmer until fully done.
9. Enjoy.

Szechwan Shrimp

Prep Time: 10 mins
Total Time: 20 mins

Servings per Recipe:	4
Calories	142 kcal
Carbohydrates	6.7 g
Cholesterol	164 mg
Fat	4.4 g
Protein	18.3 g
Sodium	500 mg

Ingredients

- 4 tbsps water
- 2 tbsps ketchup
- 1 tbsp soy sauce
- 2 tsps cornstarch
- 1 tsp honey
- 1/2 tsp crushed red pepper
- 1/4 tsp ground ginger
- 1 tbsp vegetable oil
- 1/4 cup sliced green onions
- 4 cloves garlic, minced
- 12 ounces cooked shrimp, tails removed

Directions

1. Combine water, crushed red pepper, ketchup, soy sauce, cornstarch, honey and ground ginger in a medium sized bowl and set it aside.
2. Cook green onions and garlic in hot oil for about 30 seconds before adding shrimp and mixing it well.
3. Now add sauce and cook until you see that the sauce has thickened.
4. Serve.

BASIL
Shrimp

🥣 Prep Time: 25 mins
🕒 Total Time: 1 hr 30 mins

Servings per Recipe: 9
Calories   206 kcal
Carbohydrates   2.4 g
Cholesterol   244 mg
Fat   10.2 g
Protein   25 g
Sodium   426 mg

Ingredients

2 1/2 tbsps olive oil
1/4 cup butter, melted
1 1/2 lemons, juiced
3 tbsps Dijon mustard (such as Grey Poupon Country Mustard™)
1/2 cup minced fresh basil leaves
3 cloves garlic, minced

salt to taste
white pepper
3 pounds fresh shrimp, peeled and deveined
Skewers

Directions

1. Set your grill at medium heat and put some oil on it.
2. Coat shrimp with the mixture of olive oil, mustard, melted butter, basil, lemon juice, salt, garlic and white pepper in a medium sized bowl before refrigerating it for at least one hrs.
3. Thread these shrimp into skewers.
4. Cook shrimp on the preheated grill for about four mins before transferring it to a serving dish and garnishing it with lemon wedges.

Shiitake and Potatoes

Prep Time: 15 mins
Total Time: 50 mins

Servings per Recipe: 6
Calories	223 kcal
Fat	10.9 g
Carbohydrates	28.9 g
Protein	4.1 g
Cholesterol	10 mg
Sodium	50 mg

Ingredients

- 3 tbsps olive oil
- 2 tbsps butter
- 1 lb Yukon Gold potatoes, diced
- 1/2 lb fresh shiitake mushrooms, diced
- 1 red bell pepper, diced
- 1 small acorn squash, diced
- 1 shallot, finely diced
- 2 tsps garlic powder
- 1 pinch salt
- 1 pinch ground black pepper
- 1 C. diced kale
- 4 sprigs fresh sage

Directions

1. For 3 mins stir fry the following in butter and oil: shallots, mushrooms, red pepper, potatoes, and squash. Season with: black pepper, salt, and garlic powder.
2. Let the veggie mix cook for 27 mins. Stir the contents every 3 to 5 mins. Add your sage and kale and let the contents cook for 3 more mins.
3. Enjoy.

JAPANESE
Mushroom Soup I (Shiitake, Beef, and Cheddar)

Prep Time: 10 mins
Total Time: 45 mins

Servings per Recipe: 8
Calories   163 kcal
Fat   11.4 g
Carbohydrates   5.1g
Protein   8.7 g
Cholesterol   24 mg
Sodium   809 mg

Ingredients

- 4 slices turkey bacon, diced
- 1/2 white onion, diced
- 1 lb shiitake mushrooms, sliced
- 2 cloves garlic, diced
- black pepper to taste
- 2 leaves fresh sage, diced
- 6 C. beef broth
- 1 C. shredded Cheddar cheese

Directions

1. Fry your bacon in a big pan for 7 mins. Add in your onions and then fry for another 6 mins.
2. Now add: sage, mushrooms, pepper, and garlic. Cook this mix for 12 more mins.
3. Add the broth and get everything lightly boiling. Let the contents simmer for 10 mins with a low level of heat.
4. Finally before everything is done add in your cheese and let it melt.
5. Enjoy hot.

Japanese Mushroom Soup II (Shiitake, Miso, and Tofu)

Prep Time: 10 mins
Total Time: 20 mins

Servings per Recipe: 4
Calories   92 kcal
Fat   2.5 g
Carbohydrates   11.8 g
Protein   5.5 g
Cholesterol   0 mg
Sodium   1406 mg

Ingredients

- 4 C. vegetable broth
- 4 shiitake mushrooms, thinly sliced
- 1/4 C. miso paste
- 4 tsps soy sauce
- 1/3 C. diced firm tofu
- 2 green onions, trimmed and thinly sliced

Directions

1. Get a bowl, mix: soy sauce, and miso paste
2. Boil your broth in a big pot and then combine in your mushrooms and set the heat to its lowest level.
3. Let the mushrooms lightly boil for 5 mins.
4. Now add the soy sauce mix as well as the tofu and let the contents continue to boil for 3 more mins.
5. Place your soup in serving bowls and then top with onions.
6. Enjoy.

RUSTIC BEEF
with Mushroom Sauce

🥘 Prep Time: 30 mins
🕐 Total Time: 50 mins

Servings per Recipe: 4
Calories   816 kcal
Fat   56 g
Carbohydrates   5.2g
Protein   64.9 g
Cholesterol   261 mg
Sodium   481 mg

Ingredients

- 4 (8 oz.) filet mignon steaks
- Kosher salt and fresh cracked pepper to taste
- 2 tbsps olive oil
- 3 tbsps unsalted butter
- 2 tbsps finely diced fresh ginger
- 1 tbsp finely diced garlic
- 1/2 C. thinly sliced fresh shiitake mushrooms
- 1/2 tsp kosher salt
- 3 tbsps water
- 2 tbsps white grape juice
- 1/2 C. unsalted butter
- 1 tbsp finely diced garlic chives

Directions

1. Set your oven to 400 degrees before doing anything else.
2. Sear your steaks in olive oil for 4 mins per side after seasoning them with pepper and salt.
3. Now bake everything in the oven for 12 mins. Then place the steaks to the side.
4. Get a bowl, mix: grape juice, and water
5. Stir fry your ginger and garlic in 3 tbsp of butter for 3 mins. Combine in: half a tsp of salt, and mushrooms.
6. Cook the mushrooms for 5 mins before adding the grape juice mix and letting it cook down until half of the liquid has evaporated.
7. Now add half a C. of butter.
8. Melt down the butter and with a lower level of heat let the butter get brown. This should occur in 9 mins. Add the chives and your preferred amount of pepper and salt.
9. Top your steak with the brown mushroom sauce. Enjoy.

Elegant Shiitake and Pasta

- Prep Time: 10 mins
- Total Time: 20 mins

Servings per Recipe: 4
Calories	301 kcal
Fat	16.3 g
Carbohydrates	28.4 g
Protein	7.5 g
Cholesterol	43 mg
Sodium	194 mg

Ingredients

- 6 oz. angel hair pasta
- 6 oz. fresh sliced shiitake mushrooms
- 1 clove garlic, diced
- 1/2 onion, diced
- 1/4 C. vegetable broth
- 1 tbsp olive oil
- 1/4 C. chicken broth
- 1/2 C. heavy whipping cream
- salt to taste
- ground black pepper to taste
- 2 tbsps grated Parmesan cheese
- 2 tbsps diced fresh parsley

Directions

1. Boil your pasta in water and salt for 7 to 10 mins. Remove all the liquids and set aside.
2. Stir fry your onions and garlic until aromatic then add in the mushrooms, and broth.
3. Cook the mix until half of the liquid has evaporated. Then add in your preferred amount of pepper and salt.
4. Add the sauce to the pasta and stir to coat everything evenly.
5. Garnish the servings with parsley and parmesan.
6. Enjoy.

OCTOBER'S
Lo-Mein

🥣 Prep Time: 45 mins
🕒 Total Time: 2 hrs 15 mins

Servings per Recipe: 4
Calories	603 kcal
Fat	14.9 g
Carbohydrates	78.9 g
Protein	38.3 g
Cholesterol	62 mg
Sodium	2177 mg

Ingredients

- 4 skinless, boneless chicken breast halves - cut into thin strips
- 5 tsps white sugar, divided
- 3 tbsps rice vinegar
- 1/2 C. soy sauce, divided
- 1 1/4 C. chicken broth
- 1 C. water
- 1 tbsp sesame oil
- 1/2 tsp ground black pepper
- 2 tbsps cornstarch
- 1 (12 oz.) package uncooked linguine pasta
- 2 tbsps vegetable oil, divided
- 2 tbsps diced fresh ginger root
- 1 tbsp diced garlic
- 1/2 lb fresh shiitake mushrooms, stemmed and sliced
- 6 green onions, sliced diagonally into 1/2 inch pieces

Directions

1. Boil your pasta in water and salt for 7 to 10 mins until al dente. Drain the liquid and set aside.
2. Get a bowl, mix: 1.4 C. soy sauce, 1.5 tsps sugar, and 1.5 tbsps vinegar. Add in your chicken, and cover the bowl with some plastic. Place everything in the fridge for 2 hrs. Get a 2nd bowl, mix: sesame oil, broth, black pepper, water and the remaining sugar.
3. Get a 3rd bowl, mix: cornstarch, and some of the sesame mix.
4. Combine both bowls (2nd and 3rd).
5. Now begin to stir fry your chicken for 6 mins in veggie oil in a wok. Set aside. Then add in more veggie oil and stir fry your onions, ginger, mushrooms, and garlic for 1 min.
6. Add the cornstarch mix, and cook for 3 to 5 mins until it becomes thick.
7. Finally add the noodles to the mix and make sure all the noodles are coated evenly with sauce. Enjoy.

Herbed Dumplings

Prep Time: 5 mins
Total Time: 20 mins

Servings per Recipe: 6
Calories   194 kcal
Carbohydrates   16.3 g
Cholesterol   35 mg
Fat   6.9 g
Protein   15.8 g
Sodium   367 mg

Ingredients

- 1 1/2 cups all-purpose flour
- 1 tsp salt
- 1 tsp baking soda
- 2 tsps baking powder
- 1 tsp dried thyme
- 1 tsp dried parsley
- 1 tsp dried oregano
- 3 tbsps butter
- 3/4 cup milk

Directions

1. Combine flour, salt, baking powder, thyme, baking soda, parsley and oregano in a medium sized bowl before adding butter into it.
2. Mix it well and then add milk until you find it smooth.
3. Now using a tbsp, spoon into hot soup or stew and cook it for about 15 mins before serving it.

RHUBARB
Dumplings

🍲 Prep Time: 15 mins
⏰ Total Time: 55 mins

Servings per Recipe: 10
Calories   275 kcal
Carbohydrates   36 g
Cholesterol   25 mg
Fat   13.9 g
Protein   2.6 g
Sodium   408 mg

Ingredients

- 1 (12 ounce) can refrigerated buttermilk biscuit dough
- 2 cups chopped fresh rhubarb
- 1 cup white sugar
- 1 cup water
- 1/2 cup butter, melted
- 1 1/4 tsps vanilla extract
- 1/4 tsp ground cinnamon, or to taste

Directions

1. Set your oven to 350 degrees F before doing anything else.
2. Make 3 inch circles from the biscuits and then fold it around rhubarb placed at its center.
3. Now place these dumplings in a baking dish and then pour a mixture of sugar, vanilla, water and butter over it before sprinkling some cinnamon.
4. Now bake this for about 40 mins in a preheated oven or until you see that the biscuits are golden brown.

Mexi-Melt

Prep Time: 10 mins
Total Time: 30 mins

Servings per Recipe: 6
Calories   407 kcal
Carbohydrates   40 g
Cholesterol   42 mg
Fat   20.7 g
Protein   19.3 g
Sodium   853 mg

Ingredients

1/2 (14.5 oz.) package tortilla chips, divided
1 (8 oz.) package shredded 2% Mexican cheese blend, divided
1 (15 oz.) can black beans, rinsed and drained, divided
1/2 sweet onion, chopped
1/2 (7 oz.) can green salsa (salsa verde)
1/2 (7 oz.) can salsa casera
1 (8 oz.) container reduced-fat sour cream
1 lime, cut into wedges

Directions

1. Set your oven to 400 degrees F before doing anything else.
2. Layer your baking dish with tortilla chips, half of the Mexican cheese blend and then black beans.
3. Repeat the layering process until all ingredients have been used.
4. Bake in the preheated oven for about 20 mins before pouring some sour cream over it.
5. Garnish with lime wedges.
6. Serve.

CREAM of Hash Browns Casserole

Prep Time: 15 mins
Total Time: 60 mins

Servings per Recipe: 10
Calories   272 kcal
Carbohydrates   24 g
Cholesterol   38 mg
Fat   22.2 g
Protein   7.3 g
Sodium   544 mg

Ingredients

2 (10.75 oz.) can condensed cream of chicken soup
1 1/2 C. sour cream
2 tbsps butter, softened
2 tbsps dried minced onion flakes
ground black pepper to taste
1 (2 lb) package frozen shredded hash brown potatoes, thawed
4 oz. extra sharp Cheddar cheese, shredded
1/2 C. mashed cornflakes cereal

Directions

1. Set your oven to 350 degrees F before doing anything else.
2. Combine soup, sour cream, half of your cheese, butter, hash browns, dried onion flakes, and pepper in a bowl very thoroughly before pouring it into a baking dish.
3. Bake in the preheated oven for about 45 mins.
4. Serve.

Buttery Celery and Carrots

Prep Time: 15 mins
Total Time: 45 mins

Servings per Recipe: 6
Calories   331 kcal
Carbohydrates   23.1 g
Cholesterol   61 mg
Fat   24.6 g
Protein   6 g
Sodium   909 mg

Ingredients

5 C. sliced carrots
3 tbsps butter
1 onion, chopped
1 (10.75 oz.) can condensed cream of celery soup
salt and pepper to taste

1/2 C. cubed processed cheese
2 C. seasoned croutons
1/3 C. melted butter

Directions

1. Set your oven to 350 degrees F before doing anything else.
2. Cook carrots in boiling water for 8 mins before draining.
3. Now cook onions in hot butter for a few mins and then add soup, cheese, pepper, salt and cooked carrots before transferring all this to the baking dish.
4. Spread croutons coated with melted butter over the mixture.
5. Bake in the preheated oven for about 30 mins.
6. Serve.

CREAMED Corn Bread Casserole

🥣 Prep Time: 10 mins
🕐 Total Time: 50 mins

Servings per Recipe: 6
Calories   469 kcal
Carbohydrates   45.8 g
Cholesterol   54 mg
Fat   30.7 g
Protein   7 g
Sodium   1189 mg

Ingredients

- 1 C. margarine, melted
- 2 (15.25 oz.) cans creamed corn
- 2 eggs, beaten
- 1 (8 oz.) package dry corn bread mix
- 1 onion, finely chopped
- salt and pepper to taste

Directions

1. Set your oven to 350 degrees F before doing anything else.
2. Combine everything thoroughly and pour into a baking dish before covering it up with aluminum foil.
3. Bake in the preheated oven for about 40 mins.
4. Serve.

Pumpkin Bread I

Prep Time: 15 mins
Total Time: 1 hr 15 mins

Servings per Recipe: 24
Calories   189
Fat   6.9 g
Cholesterol   23 mg
Sodium   221 mg
Carbohydrates   29.8 g
Protein   2.6 g

Ingredients

- 3 C. all-purpose flour
- 2 tsp baking soda
- ½ tsp baking powder
- 2 tsp pumpkin pie spice
- 1 tsp salt
- 3 eggs, beaten
- 2 C. white sugar
- 2/3 C. vegetable oil
- 2 C. pumpkin puree

Directions

1. Set your oven to 350 degrees F. Grease 2 (9x5-inch) loaf pans.
2. In a large bowl, mix together flour, baking soda, baking powder, pumpkin pie spice and salt.
3. In another bowl, add eggs, sugar and oil and beat till well combined.
4. Add pumpkin puree and beat till well combined.
5. Add egg mixture into flour mixture and mix till well combined.
6. Transfer the mixture in both prepared loaf pans evenly.
7. Bake for about 1 hrs or till a toothpick inserted in the center comes out clean.
8. Remove from oven and let the breads cool on wire rack before slicing.

PUMPKIN
Pie II

🥣 Prep Time: 15 mins
🕐 Total Time: 55 mins

Servings per Recipe: 8
Calories 322
Fat 11.9g
Cholesterol 79mg
Sodium 460mg
Carbohydrates 49.2g
Protein 6.5g

Ingredients

1 C. packed brown sugar
2 tsp ground cinnamon
1 tsp ground ginger
½ tsp salt
1 (15 oz.) can pumpkin puree
2 tbsp molasses
1 cup evaporated milk
3 eggs, beaten
1 (9-inch) single pie crust

Directions

1. Set your oven to 425 degrees F. Grease
2. In a large bowl, mix together brown sugar, spices.
3. Add pumpkin puree, molasses, evaporated milk and eggs and mix till well combined.
4. Transfer the mixture into pie crust.
5. Bake for about 40 mins or till set completely.

Pumpkin Soup I

 Prep Time: 15 mins
Total Time: 1 hr 10 mins

Servings per Recipe: 4
Calories   245
Fat   19.8g
Cholesterol   67mg
Sodium   899mg
Carbohydrates   16.8g
Protein   3.7g

Ingredients

- 2 small sugar pumpkins, halved and seeded
- 3 C. chicken broth
- ¾ C. heavy whipping cream
- ½ tsp ground sage, crushed
- ¼ tsp ground nutmeg
- 1½ tsp salt
- ¼ C. sour cream

Directions

1. Set your oven to 400 degrees F. Grease baking sheet.
2. Place pumpkin, cut side down onto prepared baking sheet.
3. Roast for about 45 mins. Remove the pumpkin from oven and let it cool completely.
4. After cooling, scrape out the flesh of pumpkin.
5. In a food processor, add pumpkin flesh and broth and pulse till smooth.
6. Transfer the pureed soup in a large pan on medium heat.
7. Bring to a gentle simmer. Then, stir in whipping cream, sage, nutmeg and salt till well combined.
8. Transfer the soup in serving bowls.
9. Top with the dollop of sour cream and serve hot.

PUMPKIN
Chili I

Prep Time: 15 mins
Total Time: 45 mins

Servings per Recipe: 6
Calories   285
Fat   16.6g
Cholesterol   76mg
Sodium   321mg
Carbohydrates   14.9g
Protein   21.2g

Ingredients

- 1 tbsp vegetable oil
- 1 C. onion, chopped
- 1 garlic clove, minced
- ½ C. yellow bell pepper, seeded and chopped
- ½ C. green bell pepper, seeded and chopped
- 1 lb. ground turkey
- 2 C. pumpkin puree
- 1 (14½ oz.) can diced tomatoes
- Salt, to taste
- 1½ tbsp red chili powder
- ½ tsp freshly ground black pepper
- ½ C. sour cream
- ½ C. cheddar cheese, shredded freshly

Directions

1. In a large pan, heat oil on medium heat.
2. Add onion, garlic and bell peppers and sauté for about 4-5 mins.
3. Add turkey and cook for about 5 mins or till browned.
4. Drain the excess fat from pan.
5. Now, stir in pumpkin puree, tomatoes and seasoning.
6. Bring to a gentle boil. Reduce the heat to low.
7. Simmer, covered for about 20 mins.
8. Transfer the chili to serving bowls. Top with sour cream and cheese and serve hot.

Pumpkin Curry II

Prep Time: 20 mins
Total Time: 2 hrs 15 mins

Servings per Recipe:	6
Calories	360
Fat	3.7g
Cholesterol	0mg
Sodium	244mg
Carbohydrates	64.3g
Protein	20.1g

Ingredients

- 1 C. brown lentils
- 1 C. red lentils
- ½ tsp ground turmeric
- 8 C. water
- 1 tbsp canola oil
- 1 large onion, chopped
- 3 garlic cloves, minced
- 2 tomatoes, seeded and chopped
- 2 C. pumpkin, peeled, seeded and cubed into 1-inch size
- 2 carrots, peeled and chopped
- 2 potatoes, scrubbed and chopped
- 1½ tbsp curry powder
- ¼ tsp ground cloves
- 2 tsp ground cumin
- ½ tsp salt
- ½ tsp freshly ground black pepper
- 1 granny smith apple, cored and chopped
- 2 C. packed fresh spinach, torn

Directions

1. In a pan, add both lentils, turmeric and water on medium-low heat.
2. Cover and cook for about 45 mins.
3. Drain well but reserve 2½ cups of cooking liquid.
4. In a large pan, heat oil on medium heat.
5. Add onion and sauté for about 4-5 mins.
6. Add garlic and tomatoes and cook, stirring occasionally for about 4-5 mins.
7. Stir in cooked lentils, reserved cooking liquid, pumpkin, carrots, potatoes, curry powder and spices.
8. Bring to a gentle boil. Reduce the heat to medium-low. Cook, covered for about 35-45 mins.
9. Stir in apple and spinach and simmer for about 15 mins further.
10. Season with salt and black pepper if desired.

PUMPKIN
& Chicken

🥣 Prep Time: 15 mins
🕐 Total Time: 45 mins

Servings per Recipe: 4
Calories   266
Fat   14.1g
Cholesterol   42mg
Sodium   70mg
Carbohydrates   21.2g
Protein   17.5g

Ingredients

2 (6 oz.) skinless, boneless chicken breasts, cut into bite-sized pieces
1 tsp poultry seasoning
1 tbsp olive oil
1 tbsp butter
1 onion, chopped
1 (1-inch) piece fresh ginger, chopped finely
2 garlic cloves, minced
1 tbsp ground cumin
1 tbsp ground cumin

1 tsp red pepper flakes, crushed
Pinch of ground turmeric
1 (2 lb.) sugar pumpkin, peeled, seeded and cubed
1½ C. chicken broth
½ C. canned coconut milk
Salt, to taste

Directions

1. Coat the chicken poultry seasoning completely. Keep aside for about 5 mins.
2. In a large skillet, heat oil on medium heat.
3. Add chicken and cook for about 4-5 mins. Transfer the chicken into a bowl and keep aside.
4. In the same skillet, melt butter on medium heat.
5. Add onion and sauté for about 3-4 mins. Add ginger, garlic and spices and sauté for about 1 minute. Stir in pumpkin, broth, coconut milk and cooked chicken and bring to a boil. Cook, covered for about 15-20 mins or till desired thickness. Season with salt and remove from heat. Serve hot.

Cranberry Salad

Prep Time: 20 mins
Total Time: 25 mins

Servings per Recipe: 6
Calories	338
Fat	27.1g
Cholesterol	8mg
Sodium	207mg
Carbohydrates	22.1g
Protein	6.7g

Ingredients

For Salad:
- ½ C. walnuts chopped
- ½ C. dried cranberries
- 1 bunch fresh spinach, torn
- 1 avocado, peeled, pitted and chopped
- 2 tomatoes, chopped
- ½ of red onion, sliced thinly
- ½ C. blue cheese, crumbled

For Dressing:
- 1/3 C. walnut oil
- 2 tbsp red vinegar
- 2 tbsp red raspberry jam (with seeds)
- Salt and freshly ground black pepper, to taste

Directions

1. Set your oven to 375 degrees F.
2. Place walnuts onto a large baking sheet in a single layer.
3. Toast for about 5 mins. Remove from oven and let them cool completely.
4. In a large bowl, mix together all salad ingredients.
5. In another bowl, add all dressing ingredients and beat till well combined.
6. Pour dressing over salad and toss to coat well.
7. Serve immediately.

SPINACH
Salad

🥣 Prep Time: 10 mins
🕐 Total Time: 20 mins

Servings per Recipe: 8
Calories   338
Fat   23.5g
Cholesterol   4mg
Sodium   58mg
Carbohydrates   30.4g
Protein   4.9g

Ingredients

For Salad:
1 tbsp butter
¾ C. almonds, blanched and slivered
1 C. dried cranberries
1 lb. fresh spinach, torn
For Dressing:
½ C. vegetable oil
¼ C. cider vinegar
¼ C. white vinegar
½ C. white sugar

1 tbsp poppy seeds
2 tbsp sesame seeds, toasted
2 tsp onion, minced
¼ tsp paprika

Directions

1. In a medium pan, melt butter on medium heat.
2. Add almonds and cook, stirring for about 5-10 mins
3. Remove from heat and let them cool completely.
4. In a large bowl, mix together almonds, cranberries and spinach.
5. In another bowl, add all dressing ingredients and beat till well combined.
6. Pour dressing over salad and toss to coat well.
7. Serve immediately.

Crock Pot Oatmeal I

Prep Time: 15 mins
Total Time: 6 hrs 15 mins

Servings per Recipe: 6
Calories   208 kcal
Fat   5.6 g
Carbohydrates   37.2g
Protein   3.9 g
Cholesterol   10 mg
Sodium   35 mg

Ingredients

- 1 C. steel cut oats
- 3 1/2 C. water
- 1 C. peeled and chopped apple
- 1/2 C. raisins
- 2 tbsps butter
- 1 tbsp ground cinnamon
- 2 tbsps brown sugar
- 1 tsp vanilla extract

Directions

1. For 7 hrs on low cook the following in your crock pot: vanilla extract, oats, brown sugar, water, cinnamon, apples, butter, and raisins.
2. Enjoy with milk.

CRANBERRY
Maple Oatmeal

🥣 Prep Time: 5 mins
🕐 Total Time: 15 mins

Servings per Recipe: 6
Calories 379 kcal
Fat 10.4 g
Carbohydrates 63.1g
Protein 11.6 g
Cholesterol 2 mg
Sodium 212 mg

Ingredients

- 3 1/2 C. plain or vanilla soy milk
- 1/4 tsp salt
- 2 C. rolled oats
- 1/4 C. pure maple syrup
- 1/3 C. raisins
- 1/3 C. dried cranberries
- 1/3 C. sweetened flaked coconut
- 1/3 C. chopped walnuts
- 1 (8 oz.) container plain yogurt (optional)
- 3 tbsps honey (optional)

Directions

1. Boil your milk in a large pan. Then combine in cranberries, oats, raisins, and maple syrup.
2. Let this cook, boiling, for 6 mins. Then shut off the heat and add in your coconuts and walnuts.
3. Before eating add a dollop of honey and yogurt.
4. Enjoy.

Balsamic Mushroom Sandwich

Prep Time: 8 mins
Total Time: 20 mins

Servings per Recipe: 4
Calories   445 kcal
Fat   33.4 g
Carbohydrates   31.4g
Protein   7.8 g
Cholesterol   5 mg
Sodium   426 mg

Ingredients

- 2 cloves garlic, minced
- 6 tbsps olive oil
- 1/2 tsp dried thyme
- 2 tbsps balsamic vinegar
- salt and pepper to taste
- 4 large Portobello mushroom caps
- 4 hamburger buns
- 1 tbsp capers
- 1/4 C. mayonnaise
- 1 tbsp capers, drained
- 1 large tomato, sliced
- 4 leaves lettuce

Directions

1. Preheat your broiler and set its rack so that it is near the heating source before doing anything else.
2. Get a bowl and mix: pepper, garlic, salt, olive oil, vinegar, and thyme.
3. Get a 2nd bowl, combine: mayo and capers.
4. Coat your mushrooms with half of the dressing.
5. Then toast the veggies for 5 mins under the broiler.
6. Flip the mushrooms after coating the opposite side with the remaining dressing. Toast everything for 5 more mins.
7. Now also toast your bread. Apply some mayo to the bread before layering a mushroom, some lettuce and tomato.
8. Enjoy.

MEAT LOAF
with Oats

🥣 Prep Time: 10 mins
🕐 Total Time: 1 hr 10 mins

Servings per Recipe: 1
Calories   265 kcal
Carbohydrates   18.1 g
Cholesterol   111 mg
Fat   12.9 g
Protein   18.7 g
Sodium   496 mg

Ingredients

1 lb ground beef
1 1/2 C. rolled oats
1 can French onion soup
2 eggs, beaten

Directions

1. Set your oven to 375 degrees before doing anything else.
2. Get a bowl, mix: beaten eggs, onion soup, oats, and beef.
3. Put everything into your loaf pan.
4. Bake for 1 hrs and 20 mins. Ensure the internal temperature of the meat loaf 160 degrees before removing from oven.
5. Enjoy.

Irish Apple Mash

Prep Time: 15 mins
Total Time: 40 mins

Servings per Recipe: 6
Calories	293 kcal
Fat	8.9 g
Carbohydrates	51g
Protein	5.6 g
Cholesterol	25 mg
Sodium	457 mg

Ingredients

- 2 C. water, divided
- 1 tsp brown sugar
- 1 small lemon, halved and juiced, halves reserved
- 1 large apple (such as Honey Crisp), peeled and chopped
- 4 large baking potatoes, peeled and chopped
- 6 C. water
- 3 tbsp butter
- 3 tbsp heavy whipping cream
- 1 tsp salt
- 1 tbsp ground black pepper

Directions

1. In a pan, mix together the apple, reserved lemon halves, brown sugar, lemon juice and 2 C. of the water on medium-high heat.
2. Boil for about 10-12 mins and drain well, then transfer into a large bowl.
3. Discard the lemon halves and keep the apple slices warm by covering them with foil.
4. In a large pan, add the potatoes and 6 C. of the water on medium-high heat.
5. Cook everything for 15-20 mins and drain well.
6. Add the potatoes in the bowl with the apple and with a hand blender mash them completely.

THANKSGIVING
Favorite Apple Dessert

Prep Time: 10 mins
Total Time: 30 mins

Servings per Recipe: 8
Calories	153 kcal
Fat	3.1 g
Carbohydrates	30.7g
Protein	2 g
Cholesterol	8 mg
Sodium	84 mg

Ingredients

- 2 large sweet potatoes, peeled and diced
- 2 large Honeycrisp apples, diced
- 2 tsp ground cinnamon
- 1/2 tsp ground nutmeg
- 2/3 C. water
- 2 tbsp butter, diced

Directions

1. Set your oven to 425 degrees F before doing anything else.
2. In the bottom of a microwave safe loaf pan, arrange the sweet potatoes and apples and sprinkle them with nutmeg and cinnamon.
3. Add enough water to cover about 1/2-inch of the bottom and cook everything in the microwave for about 8 mins.
4. Drain well.
5. Place the butter over the apple mixture in the shape of dots and cook everything in the oven for about 10 mins.

Traditional Autumn Sweet Treat

Prep Time: 35 mins
Total Time: 1 hr

Servings per Recipe: 8
Calories   298 kcal
Fat   6.5 g
Carbohydrates   60.7 g
Protein   2.5 g
Cholesterol   15 mg
Sodium   49 mg

Ingredients

- 4 1/2 C. peeled, cored and sliced apples
- 2 tsp lemon juice
- 2 tbsp water
- 3/4 C. brown sugar
- 3/4 C. all-purpose flour
- 3/4 C. rolled oats
- 4 tbsp butter

Directions

1. Set your oven to 350 degrees F before doing anything else and lightly, grease a casserole dish.
2. Place the apple slices in the bottom of the prepared casserole dish evenly.
3. In a bowl, mix together the water and lemon juice and drizzle over the apple slices evenly.
4. In another bowl, add the remaining ingredients and mix till a coarse crumb forms.
5. Spread the crumb mixture over the apple slices evenly and cook everything in the oven for about 25 mins.

REFRESHING
Apple Juice

🥣 Prep Time: 10 mins
🕒 Total Time: 10 mins

Servings per Recipe: 1
Calories	277 kcal
Fat	1.3 g
Carbohydrates	68.6g
Protein	4 g
Cholesterol	0 mg
Sodium	266 mg

Ingredients

4 carrots, trimmed
2 apples, quartered
2 stalks celery
1 (1/2 inch) piece fresh ginger

Directions

1. In a juicer, add all the ingredients except the ginger and process according to manufacturer's directions.
2. Add the ginger and process again.

Shrimp Tempura

Prep Time: 45 mins
Total Time: 1 hr

Servings per Recipe: 8
Calories	574 kcal
Carbohydrates	15.7 g
Cholesterol	124 mg
Fat	48.3 g
Protein	11.4 g
Sodium	424 mg

Ingredients

- 1/2 cup fish broth
- 1/4 tsp salt
- 1/2 pound fresh shrimp, peeled and deveined
- 2 quarts oil for deep frying
- 1/4 cup all-purpose flour
- 1/3 cup ice water
- 1/4 cup cornstarch
- 1 egg yolk
- 1/4 tsp salt
- 1/4 tsp white sugar
- 1 tsp shortening
- 1/2 tsp baking powder

Directions

1. Coat shrimp with the mixture of broth and salt before refrigerating for at least 20 mins.
2. Combine all-purpose flour, white sugar, ice water, cornstarch, egg yolk, salt, shortening and baking powder in a medium sized bowl.
3. Coat shrimp with this flour mixture before deep frying it in the hot oil for about 2 mins or until you see that it is golden brown from all sides.
4. Drain with the help of paper towel.
5. Serve.

CLOVES, ALLSPICE, and Cinnamon Chili (Ohio Style)

🍲 Prep Time: 10 mins
🕒 Total Time: 8 hrs 40 mins

Servings per Recipe: 8
Calories 427 kcal
Fat 35 g
Carbohydrates 7g
Protein 22.2 g
Cholesterol 100 mg
Sodium 659 mg

Ingredients

- 1 tbsp vegetable oil
- 1/2 C. diced onion
- 2 lbs ground beef
- 1/4 C. chili powder
- 1 tsp ground cinnamon
- 1 tsp ground cumin
- 1/4 tsp ground allspice
- 1/4 tsp ground cloves
- 1 bay leaf
- 1/2 (1 oz.) square unsweetened chocolate
- 2 (10.5 oz.) cans beef broth
- 1 (15 oz.) can tomato sauce
- 2 tbsps cider vinegar
- 1/4 tsp ground cayenne pepper
- 1/4 C. shredded Cheddar cheese

Directions

1. Stir fry your onions for 7 mins, in oil, then add in your beef and stir fry it while crumbling.
2. Season the meat with the following: red pepper, chili powder, vinegar, cinnamon, tomato sauce, cumin, broth, allspice, chocolate, cloves, and bay leaf.
3. Get everything boiling then place a lid on the pot, and let the contents gently boil for 90 mins stir the chili every 10 mins.
4. Place everything the fridge for 8 hrs then heat it back up before serving it all over the pasta.
5. Enjoy.

November
3 Bean Chili (Vegetarian Approved)

Prep Time: 10 mins
Total Time: 2 hrs 10 mins

Servings per Recipe: 8
Calories   260 kcal
Fat   2 g
Carbohydrates   52.6g
Protein   12.4 g
Cholesterol   1 mg
Sodium   966 mg

Ingredients

- 1 (19 oz.) can black bean soup
- 1 (15 oz.) can kidney beans, rinsed and drained
- 1 (15 oz.) can garbanzo beans, rinsed and drained
- 1 (16 oz.) can vegetarian baked beans
- 1 (14.5 oz.) can diced tomatoes in puree
- 1 (15 oz.) can whole kernel corn, drained
- 1 onion, diced
- 1 green bell pepper, diced
- 2 stalks celery, diced
- 2 cloves garlic, diced
- 1 tbsp chili powder, or to taste
- 1 tbsp dried parsley
- 1 tbsp dried oregano
- 1 tbsp dried basil

Directions

1. Add the following to your crock pot: garlic, chili powder, celery, parsley, soup, oregano, bell peppers, basil, kidney beans, onions, garbanzos, onions, baked beans, corn, and tomatoes. Set the slow cooker to high and cook for 3 hrs.
2. Let the chili sit for 20 mins before serving.
3. Enjoy with a dollop of sour cream.

BACKROAD
Chili

🥣 Prep Time: 15 mins
🕐 Total Time: 40 mins

Servings per Recipe: 6
Calories   489 kcal
Fat   22.4 g
Carbohydrates   49.2g
Protein   22.1 g
Cholesterol   64 mg
Sodium   997 mg

Ingredients

1 C. elbow macaroni
1 lb ground beef
1 small onion, diced
1 C. diced celery
1/2 large green bell pepper, diced
1 (15 oz.) can kidney beans, drained

2 (10.75 oz.) cans condensed tomato soup
2 (14.5 oz.) cans diced tomatoes
1/8 C. brown sugar
salt and pepper to taste

Directions

1. Boil your pasta in water for 9 mins then remove all the liquid.
2. Meanwhile boil your green pepper and celery in water for 5 mins then remove the liquid as well.
3. Now stir fry your beef until fully done and combine in the onions and cook them until they are see-through.
4. Now add in the celery mix, and: brown sugar, kidney beans, and tomato soup.
5. Simmer everything for 10 mins then shut the heat and add in some pepper and salt and the pasta.
6. Enjoy..

Chicken & Veggies Spring Rolls

Prep Time: 30 mins
Total Time: 45 mins

Servings per Recipe: 10
Calories	299 kcal
Fat	13.9 g
Carbohydrates	26.3g
Protein	16.2 g
Cholesterol	38 mg
Sodium	587 mg

Ingredients

- 1 quart oil for deep frying
- 2 (10 oz.) cans chunk chicken, drained and flaked
- 1 small onion, grated
- 1/2 C. finely shredded cabbage
- 1 small carrot, grated
- 1/4 C. barbeque sauce
- 1 dash hot pepper sauce
- 1 dash soy sauce
- 1 dash Worcestershire sauce
- 1 (14 oz.) package spring roll wrappers

Directions

1. In a large cast-iron skillet or deep fryer, heat the oil to 375 degrees F.
2. In a large bowl, mix together all the ingredients except wrappers.
3. Divide chicken mixture in the center of each wrapper.
4. Roll the wrapper around the filling and with your wet fingers brush the edges and press to seal completely.
5. Carefully, add the rolls in the skillet in batches.
6. Fry the rolls for about 5 mins or till golden brown and transfer onto paper towel lined plates to drain.

BANANA
& Brown Sugar Spring Rolls

> Prep Time: 10 mins
> Total Time: 20 mins

Servings per Recipe: 8
Calories 325 kcal
Fat 11.6 g
Carbohydrates 53.3g
Protein 3.5 g
Cholesterol 3 mg
Sodium 191 mg

Ingredients

- 2 large bananas
- 8 (7 inch square) spring roll wrappers
- 1 C. brown sugar, or to taste
- 1 quart oil for deep frying

Directions

1. In a large cast-iron skillet or deep fryer, heat the oil to 375 degrees F.
2. Slice the bananas in half lengthwise and cut into fourths crosswise.
3. Arrange 1 piece of banana over the corner of a spring roll wrapper diagonally and sprinkle with brown sugar.
4. Roll the each corner of the wrapper to the center and fold bottom and top corners in and continue rolling.
5. With your wet fingers brush the edges of the wrapper to seal the roll.
6. Carefully, add the banana rolls in the skillet in batches.
7. Fry the rolls till golden brown and transfer onto paper towel lined plates to drain.

Shrimp & Veggies Spring Rolls with Dipping Sauce

Prep Time: 20 mins
Total Time: 50 mins

Servings per Recipe: 6
Calories   59 kcal
Fat   0.3 g
Carbohydrates   8.9 g
Protein   3.4 g
Cholesterol   20 mg
Sodium   168 mg

Ingredients

- 6 spring roll wrappers
- 12 medium shrimp, cooked and shelled
- 1 C. shredded leaf lettuce
- 1/3 C. chopped cilantro
- 1/2 C. peeled, seeded, chopped cucumber
- 1 medium carrot, julienned

Quick Thai Dipping Sauce:
- 1 tbsp light soy sauce
- 1 tbsp white vinegar or rice vinegar
- 3 tbsps white grape juice
- 1/4 tsp grated ginger root (optional)

Directions

1. Soak the wrappers, one by one in a bowl of chilled water till limp and transfer onto a smooth surface.
2. In the center of each wrapper, place lettuce, followed by shrimp, cucumber, carrot and cilantro evenly.
3. Roll the wrapper around the filling and with your wet fingers brush the edges and press to seal completely.
4. Place the wrappers onto a large plate and with plastic wrap, cover the rolls and refrigerate before serving.
5. Meanwhile for the dipping sauce in a bowl mix together all the ingredients.
6. Serve the rolls with sauce.

APPLE
Dumplings

Prep Time: 20 mins
Total Time: 1 hr 5 mins

Servings per Recipe: 16
Calories 333 kcal
Fat 19 g
Carbohydrates 38.5g
Protein 2.7 g
Cholesterol 31 mg
Sodium 360 mg

Ingredients

2 large Granny Smith apples, peeled, cored and cut each apple in 8 wedges
2 (10 oz.) cans refrigerated crescent roll dough
1 C. butter
1 1/2 C. white sugar
1 tsp ground cinnamon
1 (12 fluid oz.) can Mountain Dew

Directions

1. Set your oven to 350 degrees F before doing anything else and grease a 13x9-inch baking dish.
2. Separate the crescent roll dough into triangles.
3. Place 1 apple wedge over a dough piece and roll the triangle around the apple wedge.
4. With your hands, pinch to seal the roll.
5. Arrange the dumplings onto the prepared baking dish in a single layer.
6. In a small pan, melt the butter and add the cinnamon and sugar and stir to combine.
7. Place the butter mixture over the dumplings evenly and top with the Mountain Dew.
8. Cook everything in the oven for about 35-45 mins..

Elegant Apple & Cheddar Stuffed Chicken Breast

Prep Time: 15 mins
Total Time: 40 mins

Servings per Recipe: 4
Calories   139 kcal
Fat   5.1 g
Carbohydrates   4.9 g
Protein   15 g
Cholesterol   46 mg
Sodium   120 mg

Ingredients

- 2 skinless, boneless chicken breasts
- 1/2 C. chopped apple
- 2 tbsp shredded Cheddar cheese
- 1 tbsp Italian-style dried bread crumbs
- 1 tbsp butter
- 1/4 C. chicken broth
- 1/4 C. water
- 1 tbsp water
- 1 1/2 tsp cornstarch
- 1 tbsp chopped fresh parsley, for garnish

Directions

1. In a bowl, mix together the apple, breadcrumbs and cheese.
2. Place the chicken breasts between 2 sheets of wax paper and with a meat mallet, flatten to 1/4-inch thickness.
3. Place the mixture in the center of the chicken breasts evenly.
4. Roll each breast around the filling and secure with the toothpicks.
5. In a large skillet, melt the butter on medium heat and cook the chicken breasts till browned completely.
6. Add the broth and 1/4 C. of the water and simmer, covered for about 15-20 mins.
7. Transfer the chicken breasts onto a plate.
8. In a bowl, mix together the cornstarch and the remaining water.
9. Add the cornstarch mixture in the skillet with juices and cook till the gravy becomes thick.
10. Pour the gravy over the chicken breasts and serve with a garnishing of parsley.

EASIEST Apple Crisp

Prep Time: 20 mins
Total Time: 1 hr

Servings per Recipe: 6
Calories   361 kcal
Fat   15.6 g
Carbohydrates   55.7g
Protein   2 g
Cholesterol   41 mg
Sodium   110 mg

Ingredients

4 C. apples - peeled, cored, and sliced
1 tsp ground cinnamon
1 C. white sugar
3/4 C. all-purpose flour
1/2 C. cold butter

Directions

1. Set your oven to 350 degrees F before doing anything else and lightly, grease an 8x8-inch casserole dish.
2. Place the apple slices in the bottom of the prepared baking dish evenly.
3. Sprinkle with the cinnamon and drizzle with the water evenly.
4. In a bowl, mix together the sugar and flour.
5. With a pastry cutter, cut the butter and mix till a crumbly mixture forms.
6. Place the mixture over the apple slices evenly and cook everything in the oven for about 30-40 mins.

Autumn Muffins

Prep Time: 15 mins
Total Time: 1 hr

Servings per Recipe: 18
Calories   249 kcal
Fat   8 g
Carbohydrates   42.6g
Protein   2.8 g
Cholesterol   23 mg
Sodium   182 mg

Ingredients

- 2 1/2 C. all-purpose flour
- 2 C. white sugar
- 1 tbsp pumpkin pie spice
- 1 tsp baking soda
- 1/2 tsp salt
- 2 eggs, lightly beaten
- 1 C. canned pumpkin puree
- 1/2 C. vegetable oil
- 2 C. peeled, cored and chopped apple
- 2 tbsp all-purpose flour
- 1/4 C. white sugar
- 1/2 tsp ground cinnamon
- 4 tsp butter

Directions

1. Set your oven to 350 degrees F before doing anything else and lightly, grease 18 cups of muffin trays.
2. In a large bowl, sift together 2 1/2 C. of the flour, baking soda, 2 C. of the sugar, pumpkin pie spice and salt. In another bowl, add the eggs, oil and pumpkin and beat till well combined. Add the egg mixture into the flour mixture and mix till well combined. Fold in the apples and transfer the mixture onto the prepared muffin cups evenly. In another bowl, mix together the remaining flour, sugar and cinnamon. With a pastry cutter, cut the butter and mix till a coarse crumb forms.
3. Place the mixture over each muffin evenly and cook everything in the oven for about 35-40 mins or till a toothpick inserted in the center comes out clean.

COUNTRYSIDE
Baked Chicken

🥣 Prep Time: 30 mins
🕐 Total Time: 2 hrs 30 mins

Servings per Recipe: 6
Calories   495 kcal
Fat   32 g
Carbohydrates   2.4g
Protein   46.6 g
Cholesterol   153 mg
Sodium   713 mg

Ingredients

2 tbsps butter
1 (4 lb) whole chicken
salt and pepper to taste
1 tsp dried thyme
2 carrots, cut in chunks
paprika to taste
8 slices turkey bacon
2 C. beef broth

Directions

1. Set your oven to 450 degrees before doing anything else.
2. Coat your chicken with the following: thyme, butter, paprika, pepper, and salt.
3. Fill the chicken with the carrots and then string the legs together.
4. Place your bacon on top of the chicken and then run toothpicks through it to keep the bacon in place.
5. Place the chicken in a roasting pan and then pour the broth around the chicken and not on top of it.
6. Cook everything for 17 mins in the oven then set the heat to 350 and continue cooking for 80 more mins. Try to baste the chicken at least 4 times while roasting.
7. Now take off the bacon from the chicken and baste it one more before cooking in the oven again to get the skin brown and crispy. This should take about 10 to 15 more mins.
8. Enjoy.

Turkey Pot Pie

Prep Time: 30 mins
Total Time: 1 hr 20 mins

Servings per Recipe: 6	
Calories	566 kcal
Fat	34.4 g
Carbohydrates	36 g
Protein	30.5 g
Cholesterol	130 mg
Sodium	1036 mg

Ingredients

- cooking spray
- 1 1/2 lbs russet potatoes, peeled and cut into 1 1/2-inch thick slices
- 6 tbsps butter, cut into pieces
- 1 C. milk
- salt and pepper, to taste
- 1 tbsp vegetable oil
- 1 lb ground turkey
- 1 medium onion, diced
- 2 (1 oz.) packages instant chicken gravy mix
- 1 C. water
- 1 (16 oz.) package frozen peas and carrots, thawed
- 2 C. shredded cheese, your preferred type

Directions

1. Coat a casserole dish with nonstick spray or oil then set your oven to 350 degrees before doing anything else.
2. Boil your potatoes for 30 mins and then remove all liquids and mash them.
3. Add in with the potatoes: pepper, butter, salt, and milk. Mash the potatoes again to mix everything in.
4. Stir fry your onions and turkey in 1 tbsp of oil until the turkey is cooked.
5. Combine with the turkey your water and gravy the pepper and salt.
6. Heat the gravy until simmering. Let the gravy simmer until it nice and thick.
7. Put the turkey in the casserole dish then add in your carrots and peas, and finally cover everything with your potatoes.
8. The final layer should be cheese.
9. Cook the dish in the oven for 30 mins. Enjoy after letting the casserole sit for 10 mins.

AU Gratin

🥣 Prep Time: 10 mins
🕐 Total Time: 40 mins

Servings per Recipe: 9
Calories   263 kcal
Fat   9.6 g
Carbohydrates   37.7g
Protein   7 g
Cholesterol   19 mg
Sodium   739 mg

Ingredients

Unsalted butter
2 1/2 C. chicken broth
4 large russet potatoes, peeled, diced
1 tsp salt
1/4 C. unsalted butter
4 cloves garlic, finely chopped
1/2 C. grated Parmesan cheese
Salt and pepper to taste
1/2 C. panko bread crumbs

Directions

1. Coat a baking dish with butter then set your oven to 375 degrees before doing anything else.
2. Add your broth to a large pot and combine in 1 tsp of salt and your potatoes.
3. Get everything boiling.
4. Once the potatoes are boiling, place a lid on the pot, set the heat to low, and let everything cook for 15 mins.
5. Remove the potatoes from the liquid to a bowl.
6. Place the broth in a separate bowl as well.
7. Clean the pot then add in 2 tbsps of butter and begin to stir fry your garlic in it for 4 mins.
8. Add the potatoes into the pot and mash them with the butter and garlic.
9. Add in 1 C. of broth and continue mashing.
10. Now stir in the 1/4 C. of cheese and more 2 tbsp of butter.
11. Add some pepper and salt if you like.
12. Spread the potatoes into the baking dish and top it with the rest of the cheese and the bread crumbs.
13. Cook everything in the oven for 25 mins. Enjoy.

Creamy Mashed Potatoes

Prep Time: 10 mins
Total Time: 30 mins

Servings per Recipe: 6	
Calories	212 kcal
Fat	10 g
Carbohydrates	27.5g
Protein	4.3 g
Cholesterol	26 mg
Sodium	136 mg

Ingredients

- 2 lbs potatoes, scrubbed and chopped
- 2 tbsps butter
- 2 oz. cream cheese
- 1/3 C. sour cream
- 2 tsps dried basil
- 1/2 tsp garlic powder
- salt and ground black pepper to taste

Directions

1. Get your potatoes boiling in water and salt, place a lid on the pot, set the heat to low, and let everything cook for 25 mins.
2. Remove all the liquid and being to partially mash your potatoes.
3. Add in: the garlic powder, butter, basil, cream cheese, and sour cream.
4. Mash the potatoes until they are smooth then add in some pepper and salt.
5. Enjoy.

BUTTERY
Quinoa

🥣 Prep Time: 10 mins
🕒 Total Time: 30 mins

Servings per Recipe: 6
Calories 157 kcal
Fat 4.7 g
Carbohydrates 21.8g
Protein 6.5 g
Cholesterol 8 mg
Sodium 97 mg

Ingredients

- 1 tbsp butter
- 1 C. uncooked quinoa
- 2 C. chicken broth
- 1/4 C. chopped onion
- 1 clove garlic, minced
- 1 tsp chopped fresh thyme
- 1/2 tsp black pepper
- 3/4 C. frozen peas
- 1/2 C. grated Pecorino Romano cheese
- 2 tbsps chopped fresh parsley

Directions

1. Toast your quinoa for 3 mins in butter then add: pepper, broth, thyme, garlic, and onions.
2. Get the mix boiling then add in the peas, place a lid on the pot, lower the heat, and let the mix cook for 17 mins.
3. Now add in your parsley and Romano then stir the contents.
4. Place the quinoa in a bowl and top with some more cheese.
5. Enjoy.

Feta, Peppers, and Lime Quinoa Salad

Prep Time: 30 mins
Total Time: 1 hr 25 mins

Servings per Recipe: 8
Calories	195 kcal
Fat	9.8 g
Carbohydrates	22.1 g
Protein	6.3 g
Cholesterol	18 mg
Sodium	197 mg

Ingredients

- 1 C. quinoa
- 1 tbsp butter
- 2 C. chicken broth
- 1/2 C. diced green bell pepper
- 1/2 C. diced red onion
- 1 C. corn
- 1 (15 oz.) can black beans, drained
- 1/4 C. chopped cilantro
- 1 large tomato, diced
- 1/2 C. fresh lime juice, or to taste
- 2 tbsps red vinegar
- 2 tbsps olive oil
- 1 tbsp adobo seasoning
- 1/2 C. feta cheese
- salt and black pepper to taste

Directions

1. Get a bowl, combine: cheese, green peppers, adobo, onions, olive oil, corn, vinegar, black beans, lime, cilantro, and tomatoes.
2. Run cold water over your quinoa until it runs clear. Then toast the quinoa in butter for 4 mins.
3. Add in the broth and get it boiling.
4. Once everything is boiling, set the heat to low, and cook for 12 mins.
5. After the quinoa has cooked, add the cheese mix and also some pepper and salt. Place everything in a bowl, in the fridge, for 40 mins.
6. Enjoy.

MUSHROOM and Chard Quinoa

Prep Time: 20 mins
Total Time: 40 mins

Servings per Recipe: 8
Calories   224 kcal
Fat   4.7 g
Carbohydrates   36.6 g
Protein   9.6 g
Cholesterol   0 mg
Sodium   323 mg

Ingredients

- 1 tbsp olive oil
- 1 onion, diced
- 3 cloves garlic, minced
- 2 C. uncooked quinoa, rinsed
- 1 C. canned lentils, rinsed
- 8 oz. fresh mushrooms, chopped
- 1 quart vegetable broth
- 1 bunch Swiss chard, stems removed, shredded

Directions

1. Stir fry your garlic and onions for 7 mins in oil.
2. Now add: mushrooms, lentils, and quinoa.
3. Stir and heat everything for 1 mins.
4. Now combine in your broth and get everything boiling. Once the mix is boiling reduce the heat, place a lid on the pot, and simmer the contents for 22 mins.
5. Shut the head, and add the chards. Stir the mix to evenly distribute the chards throughout the quinoa.
6. Place the lid back on the pot and let the quinoa sit for 7 mins.
7. Enjoy.

November's Quinoa

Prep Time: 5 mins
Total Time: 40 mins

Servings per Recipe: 4
Calories	196 kcal
Fat	6 g
Carbohydrates	28.9 g
Protein	6.7 g
Cholesterol	0 mg
Sodium	455 mg

Ingredients

- 1 tbsp extra-virgin olive oil
- 1 C. quinoa
- 2 C. chicken broth
- 2 tbsps soy sauce
- 1 tbsp minced fresh ginger root
- 1 clove garlic, minced
- 2 green onions, chopped

Directions

1. Stir fry your quinoa in olive oil for 4 mins then add: garlic, broth, ginger, and soy sauce.
2. Get everything boiling, place a lid on the pot, lower the heat, and cook for 27 mins.
3. Stir the quinoa and add the onions.
4. Enjoy.

Made in the USA
Las Vegas, NV
02 November 2022